Ontario and Beyond:
Discovering the beauty of East Central Canada

Table of Contents

Introduction

Welcome to Ontario, a province situated in east-central Canada, noted for its natural beauty, rich history, varied culture, and vibrant metropolitan hubs.

Ontario is the second-largest province in Canada and is bounded by the Great Lakes to the south and the Hudson Bay to the north. The terrain of Ontario is immensely diversified, with massive forests, vast freshwater lakes, and steep mountains. Tourists may discover the natural splendor of the province by trekking through its lush woods, bathing in its beautiful lakes, or skiing on its snow-covered slopes.

Ontario's climate is also very variable, with scorching summers and chilly winters. The southern half of the province enjoys a humid continental climate, while the northern sections have a subarctic environment. Ontario's climate makes it the ideal place for year-round outdoor sports and excursions.

Ontario has a rich and intriguing history, with its oldest human occupants reaching back almost 10,000 years ago. The province was formerly populated by several Indigenous communities, including the Anishinaabe, Haudenosaunee, and Wendat peoples. Subsequently, European explorers arrived in the 17th century, and Ontario became a British province in the 18th century. Today, Ontario is a global and diversified province, with various communities of immigrants from all over the globe.

Traveling around Ontario is simple because of its well-developed transportation system. The province has a comprehensive network of roads, buses, and railways that link its main cities and communities. Tourists may also opt to explore the province's natural beauties by hiring a vehicle, motorcycling, or trekking. Ontario is an intriguing and alluring province with attractions for every kind of traveler, from its bustling urban centers to its untamed wilderness. Ontario has something to offer everyone, regardless of interest in history, culture, environment, or adventure.

Chapter 1

Planning Your Trip

Arranging your vacation to Ontario needs careful consideration of different elements to guarantee that you have a safe and happy visit. These are some crucial elements to consider:

When to Visit

Ontario's climate fluctuates depending on the season, with scorching summers and frigid winters. The greatest time to visit Ontario is during the summer months, from June through August when the weather is pleasant and bright. Nevertheless, these months are also the busiest and most costly, so you may want to consider going during the shoulder seasons of spring and autumn when the crowds are fewer, and the rates are cheaper. If you're interested in winter sports like skiing and snowboarding, the ideal time to visit Ontario is between December and March. Nonetheless, be prepared for the cooler weather and snowfall during this season.

Entry Requirements

Visitors to Ontario must have a valid passport or other travel documentation to enter the country. If you're going from a place that needs a visa, you must get one before your trip. It's crucial to verify the newest entrance requirements before your trip to ensure that you have all the relevant documentation.

Budgeting and Money

Ontario may be an expensive location, so it's vital to manage your money wisely. Lodging, food, and transportation are the major expenditures, so consider staying in budget-friendly housing choices like hostels or Airbnb rentals. You may also save money by dining at local markets or food trucks rather than restaurants.

Accommodations

Ontario provides a broad selection of hotel alternatives to suit all budgets and interests. From luxury hotels to budget-friendly hostels and campsites, there are plenty of alternatives to pick from. If you're visiting during the high season, it's crucial to book your hotel early to prevent disappointment.

Transportation

Ontario has a comprehensive transportation network, including buses, railways, and motorways. The most convenient method to get throughout Ontario is by vehicle, but if you're going on a budget, buses, and trains are viable choices. You might also consider hiring a bike or strolling if you're touring a city or town.

It's crucial to understand that Ontario is a huge province, and distances between cities and attractions might be substantial. Be careful to include travel time when arranging your schedule.

Remember, organizing your vacation to Ontario takes careful consideration of numerous elements such as the time of year, budget, housing, and transportation. By taking these considerations into account and preparing in advance, you can guarantee that you have a safe and pleasurable journey to this lovely province

Chapter 2

Toronto

Toronto is the biggest and most populated city in Canada, situated in the province of Ontario. The city is located on the northern side of Lake Ontario and is noted for its rich culture, active arts scene, and gorgeous architecture.

As the financial capital of Canada, Toronto is a bustling metropolis with a dynamic downtown core filled with skyscrapers and bustling streets. Yet, the city also offers a gentler side, with attractive neighborhoods and green areas that give relief from the rush and bustle of the metropolis.

Toronto is home to numerous world-renowned attractions, including the CN Tower, which is one of the highest freestanding buildings in the world and gives stunning views of the city. Other prominent sites include the Royal Ontario

Museum, the Art Gallery of Ontario, and the Hockey Hall of Fame.

The city is also noted for its diversified culinary scene, with a vast choice of restaurants and cuisine options that represent the city's ethnic population. From upscale dining to street cuisine, Toronto has plenty to offer every palette and budget.

In addition to its attractions and cuisine industry, Toronto is also recognized for its thriving arts and cultural scene. The city is home to many theaters and performing arts venues, as well as festivals and events that celebrate music, dance, and visual arts. Toronto provides something for everyone.

Must-see Attractions in Toronto.
Toronto is a city that provides a wealth of intriguing attractions, each with its distinct traits that make them worth visiting. These are some of the top significant attractions in Toronto

CN Tower — Situated in the center of downtown Toronto, the CN Tower is an iconic landmark that rises over the city's skyline. This stunning tower contains an observation deck that gives amazing views of the city and Lake Ontario. Guests may also experience the EdgeWalk, an exciting adventure that lets them walk outdoors along the edge of the tower, strapped to a safety rail.

Royal Ontario Museum — Situated at 100 Queen's Park, the Royal Ontario Museum is Canada's biggest museum of foreign cultures and natural history. The museum has a broad collection of artifacts and exhibits from throughout the globe, including mummies, dinosaur bones, and more.

Art Gallery of Ontario — Situated at 317 Dundas Street West, the Art Gallery of Ontario is a major art museum that showcases a significant collection of Canadian and foreign art. The museum's collection contains works by prominent painters such as Van Gogh, Picasso, and Rembrandt.

Toronto Islands — Situated only a short boat journey from downtown Toronto, the Toronto Islands are a set of islands that provide a calm retreat from the hustle and bustle of the city. The islands have gorgeous parks, beaches, and wildlife, as well as a range of sports such as kayaking and riding.

St. Lawrence Market — Situated at 93 Front Street East, St. Lawrence Market is one of Toronto's most popular locations for foodies. The market offers over 100 exhibitors providing fresh fruit, meats, cheeses, and other specialty items.

Distillery District — Situated in Toronto's east end, the Distillery District is a pedestrian-friendly district that was originally home to a huge whiskey distillery. Currently, the neighborhood is a popular location for shopping, eating, and nightlife. Tourists may explore the district's Victorian-era buildings, cobblestone streets, and distinctive boutiques and galleries.

Ontario Science Centre — Situated at 770 Don Mills Road, the Ontario Science Centre is a fascinating and informative destination for visitors of all ages. The museum contains interactive displays and presentations that enable visitors to learn about science and technology in a hands-on approach.

Ripley's Aquarium of Canada — Situated at 288 Bremner Boulevard, Ripley's Aquarium of Canada is a must-visit destination for everyone interested in aquatic life. The aquarium contains a range of displays and environments showing marine species from throughout the globe, including sharks, rays, and jellyfish. Guests may also attend daily demonstrations and feedings.

Whether you're interested in history, art, culinary, or nature, Toronto offers something for everyone. These prominent attractions provide a sensory-invoking experience that will leave you with vivid recollections of your visit to this dynamic city.

Museums and Galleries
Toronto has a rich cultural background, and its museums and galleries reflect this variety. From ancient relics to modern art, Toronto's museums and galleries provide a sensory-invoking experience that will captivate and excite visitors of all ages and backgrounds.

The Royal Ontario Museum is a world-renowned museum that showcases a broad collection of artifacts and exhibitions from across the globe. Here, visitors may tour galleries devoted to natural history, art, and other cultures, including ancient

Egyptian mummies, dinosaur bones, and indigenous Canadian art.

The Art Gallery of Ontario is a spectacular art museum that showcases a large collection of Canadian and foreign art. The gallery's collection contains works by prominent painters such as Van Gogh, Picasso, and Rembrandt. The gallery's displays rotate periodically, so visitors may always find something new.

For individuals interested in modern art, the Museum of Contemporary Art is a must-visit location. The museum is set in a magnificent refurbished structure in the Junction Triangle district and presents exhibits of cutting-edge contemporary art from Canada and throughout the globe.

The Gardiner Museum is a sensory-invoking museum devoted to ceramics and pottery. Here, visitors may explore galleries showing ancient pottery from throughout the globe, as well as modern ceramics from Canada and beyond.

Toronto also has numerous smaller galleries that exhibit local artists and developing talent. The Power Plant Contemporary Art Gallery is a waterfront gallery that presents exhibitions of contemporary art, including multimedia works, photography, and sculpture. The AGO's sibling institution, the Art Gallery of York University, includes exhibits of contemporary art and performance, as well as public programs and artist discussions.

Shopping and Dining in Toronto

Toronto provides a varied selection of shopping and eating experiences for residents and tourists alike. From luxury shopping on Bloor Street to the trendy boutiques and restaurants of Queen Street West, there's something for everyone in Toronto.

Shopping in Toronto is an exciting experience that provides everything from high-end luxury brands to antique and artisanal products. Bloor-Yorkville is recognized as Toronto's top retail area, including high-end boutiques like Louis Vuitton, Chanel, and Gucci. The Eaton Centre, situated in the center of downtown, is a major retail mall that has over 250 businesses, including Zara, H&M, and Sephora.

If you're seeking something more unusual, the Queen Street West district is a must-visit place. Here, you'll discover a mix of independent shops and well-known brands, as well as antique stores and handcrafted items. Kensington Market is another popular location for people wanting a more varied shopping experience, featuring vintage and second-hand stores, as well as independent businesses and food vendors. Toronto is also a food lover's heaven, with a varied choice of eating alternatives to suit every taste and budget. The city's heterogeneous population has affected its cuisine scene, and you can get everything from traditional Chinese dim sum to classic Italian pasta meals. For fans of excellent cuisine, Toronto features numerous Michelin-starred restaurants, including Alo and Canoe. The city's culinary culture is also noted for its inventive and experimental cuisine, with restaurants like Antler and Actinolite pushing the limits of conventional Canadian cuisine.

If you're on a budget, Toronto also offers lots of economical and excellent choices, including food trucks and small cafes. The St. Lawrence Market is a popular destination for foodies, with over 120 exhibitors providing everything from fresh seafood to artisanal cheeses.

Nightlife & Entertainment

As the sun goes down in Toronto, the city comes alive with a dynamic nightlife and entertainment scene that appeals to a broad variety of tastes and interests. From fashionable nightclubs and live music venues to comedy clubs and theaters, Toronto offers something for everyone.

For those eager to dance the night away, Toronto's nightlife culture is world-renowned. The Entertainment District is home to some of the city's best nightclubs, including Rebel, Uniun, and Nest. These venues include prominent DJs and live music performances, state-of-the-art sound and lighting systems, and VIP spaces for those wishing to have a more exclusive experience.

If live music is more your vibe, Toronto offers a booming music culture with venues ranging from tiny intimate bars to big stadiums. The renowned Massey Hall is a must-visit site for music fans, with a long history of hosting great artists like Bob Dylan, Neil Young, and Joni Mitchell. The Danforth Music Hall is another prominent venue, showcasing a mix of indie, rock, and techno music artists.

Comedy aficionados can also find much to enjoy in Toronto, with many comedy clubs presenting regular events. The Second City is a world-renowned comedy club that has started the careers of several notable comedians, including John Candy and Mike Myers. Other popular comedy clubs include Yuk Yuk's and Absolute Comedy, which offer a mix of local and international performers.

If you wish to have a more laid-back evening, Toronto boasts various theaters that exhibit plays, musicals, and other live acts. The Royal Alexandra Theatre and the Princess of Wales Theatre are two of the city's most prominent theaters, both situated in the center of the Entertainment

District. Other significant theaters include the Ed Mirvish Theatre, the Young Centre for the Performing Arts, and the Canadian Stage Company.

Toronto is also home to various unique entertainment experiences, including escape rooms, speakeasies, and rooftop bars. The rec room is a popular location for individuals searching for a combination of arcade games, virtual reality experiences, and craft beer. For those searching for a more intimate experience, the Shameful Tiki Room and the Snakes and Lattes Board Game Café provide a funny and fascinating night out. Toronto's nightlife and entertainment scene is a big lure for tourists to the city, with a vast selection of alternatives to suit every taste and interest. Whether you're wanting to dance the night away, enjoy live music, or laugh out loud at a comedy club, Toronto offers something for everyone.

Parks and Outdoor activities in Toronto
Toronto is renowned for its busy metropolis, but the city also features an outstanding range of parks and outdoor activities that give a calm getaway from the hustle and bustle. These are some of the top parks and outdoor activities to discover in Toronto:

High Park - High Park is one of Toronto's biggest parks, encompassing over 400 acres of green space. The park is home to a range of leisure activities, including hiking paths, picnic spots, and sports facilities. One of the park's most popular attractions is the High Park Zoo, where visitors may observe a variety of animals, including bison, llamas, and peacocks.

Toronto Islands - The Toronto Islands are a series of tiny islands situated close to the coast of downtown Toronto. The islands are accessible by boat and provide a range of leisure activities, including beaches, biking routes, and kayaking. Guests may also enjoy Centreville Amusement Park, a small amusement park that features rides, games, and attractions for all ages.

Don Valley Trail - The Don Valley Trail is a picturesque 11-kilometer route that goes along the Don River. The route is great for hiking, cycling, and birding, and offers a calm getaway from the city's hustle and bustle. Throughout the journey, tourists may take in spectacular views of the river and the surrounding woodland countryside.

Scarborough Bluffs - The Scarborough Bluffs is a beautiful geological structure situated on the eastern outskirts of Toronto. The bluffs stand approximately 90 meters above Lake Ontario and give amazing views of the lake and the surrounding area. Tourists may trek along the bluffs or take a boat cruise to observe them from the sea.

Rouge Park - Rouge Park is one of Canada's biggest urban parks, comprising over 40 square kilometers of protected wilderness. The park is host to a range of leisure activities, including hiking, camping, and fishing. Visitors may also explore the park's marshes, woodlands, and meadows, which are home to a diversity of plant and animal species.

Evergreen Brick Works - Evergreen Brick Works is a former brick mill that has been turned into a community center for sustainability and outdoor sports. The location contains a farmers' market, bike rentals, and a range of educational events centered on sustainability and conservation.

Toronto's parks and outdoor activities provide a broad variety of possibilities to leave the city and discover the natural beauty of the region.

Chapter 3

Ottawa

Our next destination is Ottawa, the attractive and historic capital of Canada. Situated in eastern Ontario, Ottawa is a city that smoothly integrates its rich history and cultural heritage with contemporary conveniences and attractions.

In the center of Ottawa is Parliament Hill, a majestic complex of Gothic Revival buildings that serves as the seat of the Canadian government. Visitors may enjoy a guided tour of the buildings or see the Changing of the Guard ritual, which takes place every day during the summer months.

Ottawa is much more than simply politics and history. The city is also home to an amazing array of museums and galleries, including the Canadian Museum of History, the National Gallery of Canada, and the Canadian War Museum. Each of these institutions gives a distinct perspective on Canadian culture and history, and are must-see attractions for visitors to the city.

Ottawa is a paradise for foodies, with a bustling culinary scene that displays the finest of Canadian cuisine. Tourists may indulge in local favorites like poutine, beaver tails, and maple syrup, or explore the city's varied array of foreign eateries.

Ottawa comes alive with a thriving nightlife scene. From comfortable pubs to trendy cocktail bars to busy nightclubs, there's no lack of locations to spend a night out on the town, But maybe what makes Ottawa distinctive is its natural beauty. The city is located on the banks of the Ottawa River, which provides spectacular vistas and several leisure activities, including kayaking, canoeing, and cycling. And just a short drive from the city comes Gatineau Park, a large wilderness region that provides limitless chances for hiking, camping, and outdoor fun.

Must-see attractions in Ottawa

Ottawa is home to an array of attractions that exhibit the city's rich history, cultural legacy, and natural beauty. These are just a handful of the must-see sites in the nation's capital:

Parliament Hill - Situated in the center of the city, Parliament Hill is the hub of Canadian politics and a symbol of the country's democratic ideals. Tourists may enjoy guided tours of the spectacular Gothic Revival structures, including the famed Peace Tower, and see the Changing of the Guard ritual during the summer months.

Canadian Museum of History - Located across the Ottawa River in Gatineau, Quebec, the Canadian Museum of History is one of the country's most visited museums. The museum gives a comprehensive look at Canadian history, from the First Nations to current times, via interactive exhibits, artifacts, and multimedia presentations.

National Gallery of Canada - Situated only a short walk from Parliament Hill, the National Gallery of Canada exhibits an amazing collection of Canadian and foreign art. Visitors may examine works by famous painters such as Tom Thomson, Emily Carr, and the Group of Seven, as well as modern pieces by artists from across the globe.

Canadian War Museum - Another must-see museum in Ottawa, the Canadian War Museum is committed to preserving and presenting the military history of Canada. Exhibitions encompass everything from early battles to modern-day peacekeeping efforts and include items such as tanks, aircraft, and weaponry.

Rideau Canal - A UNESCO World Heritage Site, the Rideau Canal is a gorgeous 202-kilometer canal that spans from Ottawa to Kingston. Tourists may enjoy a beautiful boat tour of the canal or stroll or bike along the gorgeous trails that follow its banks.

ByWard Market - Situated in the center of downtown Ottawa, the ByWard Market is a lively outdoor market that offers more than 600 stores, restaurants, and vendors. Visitors may try local delights such as maple syrup and beaver tails, or peruse the unusual collection of crafts, jewelry, and souvenirs.

Gatineau Park - Only a short drive from downtown Ottawa, Gatineau Park is a huge wilderness region that provides infinite chances for outdoor activity. Visitors may walk, cycle, or ski along the park's paths, or swim, fish, and paddle in its beautiful lakes and rivers.

These are just a handful of the many fantastic attractions that Ottawa has to offer. With its rich history, thriving cultural scene, and spectacular natural beauty, there's no lack of things to see and do in this dynamic and hospitable city.

Museums and Galleries in Ontario
Ontario is home to some of the most magnificent museums and galleries in Canada, having huge collections that are guaranteed to engage visitors of all ages and interests. From ancient treasures to modern art, there is something for everyone to explore at the museums and galleries of Ontario.

The Royal Ontario Museum, situated in Toronto, is one of the biggest and most diversified museums in North America. The museum's collection comprises approximately six million pieces, including fossils, art, and cultural relics from throughout the globe. Guests may visit exhibitions on ancient civilizations, Canadian art, natural history, and much more. One of the most popular displays is the dinosaur gallery, which presents the greatest collection of dinosaur fossils in Canada.

The Art Gallery of Ontario, also situated in Toronto, is a must-visit for art aficionados. The gallery's collection comprises about 95,000 works of art, ranging from contemporary art to Canadian and European classics. Visitors may view the classic works of painters like Tom Thomson, the Group of Seven, and Pablo Picasso, as well as modern works by up-and-coming Canadian artists. The gallery also includes a variety of exhibits throughout the year, so there is always something new to explore.

The National Gallery of Canada, situated in Ottawa, is the country's primary art museum. The gallery's collection comprises approximately 75,000 pieces of art, including paintings, sculptures, and photos from Canada and throughout the globe. Visitors may visit galleries devoted to

Canadian art, Indigenous art, and European art, as well as special exhibits that feature works from rising artists and renowned masters.

The Canadian Museum of History, also situated in Ottawa, is Canada's most-visited museum. The museum's collection comprises approximately 4 million objects and specimens, representing Canada's rich history and culture. Visitors may examine exhibitions on First Nations history, Canadian military history, and Canadian political history. One of the most popular exhibitions is the Canadian History Hall, which gives a tour of Canada's history from the first human settlement to the current day.

The Aga Khan Museum, situated in Toronto, is a unique museum that highlights the arts and culture of Muslim civilizations from throughout the globe. The museum's collection comprises about 1,000 objects, including textiles, pottery, and manuscripts. Visitors may tour galleries devoted to Islamic art, calligraphy, and architecture, and learn about the rich cultural legacy of the Muslim world.

In conclusion, the museums and galleries of Ontario provide a plethora of chances to learn about history, culture, and art from throughout the globe. Whether you are interested in ancient civilizations or modern art, there is something for everyone to discover at the museums and galleries of Ontario.

Shopping and Dining in Ottawa

Shopping and eating in Ottawa are a must-do for every tourist in the city. From the fashionable shops of the ByWard Market to the posh malls on the city's outskirts, there is no lack of places to shop till you drop. The same applies to eating, with an abundance of restaurants and cafés dishing up exquisite food from throughout the globe.

Let's start with shopping. The ByWard Market is a must-visit place for every shopper in Ottawa. This outdoor market is the oldest in the city and is home to over 600 enterprises, including artisanal food sellers, stylish boutiques, and specialized stores. You may get anything from handcrafted jewelry and apparel to fresh food and baked delicacies.

For those searching for a more upmarket shopping experience, Ottawa's suburbs offer various malls that appeal to all interests and budgets. The Rideau Centre, situated in the center of downtown, is the biggest shopping mall in the city and has over 180 shops, including prominent fashion brands and luxury boutiques. Other malls worth checking out include Bayshore Shopping Centre in the west end and St. Laurent Shopping Centre in the east end.

When it comes to eating, Ottawa boasts an excellent culinary scene with restaurants dishing gourmet food from across the globe. For those wishing to try some of the city's top eateries, travel to the fashionable areas of Westboro and Hintonburg. These regions are home to some of the city's top-rated restaurants, including Pure Kitchen, a vegetarian restaurant recognized for its fresh and healthful meals, and Supply and Demand, an Italian-inspired restaurant serving seasonal and locally produced products. For a more informal eating experience, the ByWard Market is a terrific alternative with its vast range of cafés, bars, and restaurants. For a famous Ottawa delicacy, make sure to sample a BeaverTail, a fried pastry treat fashioned like a beaver's tail and topped with your choice of sweet toppings.

Shopping and eating in Ottawa are experiences not to be missed. Whether you're seeking unusual gifts or a tasty lunch, the city provides something for everyone.

Nightlife & Entertainment in Ottawa

The night is never silent in Ottawa, since there are lots of opportunities for entertainment once the sun sets. From live music and theatrical events to lively pubs and nightclubs, Ottawa offers something for everyone.

One famous venue for live music is the National Arts Centre, which organizes a variety of acts throughout the year, including jazz, classical music, and drama. The Canadian Tire Centre is another prominent arena, noted for holding large concerts and athletic events. For those seeking to dance the night away, there are plenty of clubs and pubs to pick from. The ByWard Market district is a popular attraction, with a variety of restaurants and nightclubs serving music and beverages late into the night.

If you're in the mood for something a bit more laid back, you may check out one of the numerous pubs in the city. The Château Lafayette, often known as "The Laff," is one of the oldest and most renowned pubs in Ottawa, featuring a comfortable environment and live music on weekends.

For those who appreciate a good chuckle, the Ottawa Comedy Nest is a popular venue for stand-up comedy, presenting both local and international talent. In addition to these possibilities, Ottawa also boasts a flourishing theatrical industry, with a variety of shows throughout the year. The National Arts Centre and the Great Canadian Theatre Company are two popular sites to see a performance.

Nevertheless, Ottawa's nightlife and entertainment industry has lots to offer tourists and residents alike, making it a terrific location for a night out on the town.

Parks and Outdoor Activities in Ottawa
Ottawa is famed for its natural beauty and abundance of open areas, making it the ideal location for outdoor lovers. From hiking and bike routes to tranquil parks and gardens, there is no lack of options to go outdoors and enjoy the fresh air.

One of the most popular outdoor locations in Ottawa is Gatineau Park, only a short drive from downtown. This park features over 361 square kilometers of protected wilderness, including routes for hiking, biking, and cross-country skiing. In the summer, visitors may swim in the park's lakes, enjoy a picnic, or take in the spectacular views from the scenic lookouts. In the autumn, the park is a famous site for leaf peeping, as the trees convert into a stunning display of oranges, yellows, and reds.

Another fantastic outdoor site in Ottawa is the Rideau Canal. This UNESCO World

Heritage Site is the world's biggest skating rink in the winter, and a popular site for boating and riding in the summer. Tourists may hire bikes or boats to explore the canal, or just take a stroll along the picturesque paths that flank the river.

For a quiet outdoor experience, the Ornamental Gardens of the Central Experimental Farm is a must-see. This large garden offers a broad range of plants and flowers, as well as various water features and sculptures. Take a walk around the gardens and enjoy the lovely smells of the flowering flowers, while feeling the cold wind on your cheeks.

For those searching for a more challenging outdoor experience, whitewater rafting on the Ottawa River is a fascinating alternative. The river provides a series of rapids for all ability levels, with professional guides to assure your safety. When you paddle over the rapids, you'll feel the rush of the cold water on your skin and the thrill of negotiating the twists and turns of the river.

Chapter 4

Niagara Falls

I'll never forget the first time I visited Niagara Falls. As I reached the falls, the sound of the water rushing down increased louder and louder until it was nearly overwhelming. I could feel the mist on my face and the water droplets on my skin. The sheer strength and size of the falls were staggering.

I stood there, watching the water cascade over the edge and into the river below, transfixed by the scene. The hues of the sea were extremely brilliant, ranging from a deep blue to a dazzling aquamarine. I couldn't take my eyes off the Horseshoe Falls, the biggest and most beautiful of the three falls. That was like nothing I had ever seen before.

As I strolled along the observation platform, I witnessed individuals of different ages and countries, each in their world, soaking in the majesty of the falls. Some were snapping photographs, others were standing in quiet, while others were speaking and joking with friends and family.

When the sun started to set, the sky became tones of orange and pink, creating a warm light over the falls. The lights lighting the falls began to sparkle, making the water appear like it was dancing. That was like a scene from a storybook, and I felt blessed to experience it in person.

From that point on, I knew that Niagara Falls would always occupy a particular place in my heart.

Being one of the world's most spectacular natural marvels, Niagara Falls draws millions of people each year. The deafening roar of the falls and the mist that rises far into the air are sights and noises that will leave you in awe. It's impossible to express the sheer size of the falls and the beauty that surrounds them unless you've seen it for yourself.

Situated on the boundary between Canada and the United States, Niagara Falls is made up of three waterfalls: the Horseshoe Falls, the American Falls, and the Bridal Veil Falls. Whether you're a nature enthusiast, a thrill-seeker, or just seeking a gorgeous escape, Niagara Falls has something to offer for everyone. From boat excursions to hiking trails to lovely restaurants and stores, you'll never run out of things to do and see. Therefore, prepare to be fascinated by the sheer force and spectacular beauty of Niagara Falls.

Must-see Attractions in Niagara Falls

Niagara Falls is one of the world's most recognized natural marvels, and it provides tourists with a broad choice of activities that are guaranteed to delight everyone. These are some of the key attractions that you don't want to miss while visiting Niagara Falls:

The Falls themselves: The major attraction, of course, is the Falls themselves. The Falls are made up of three separate waterfalls: Horseshoe Falls, American Falls, and Bridal Veil Falls. The view from the Canadian side is especially magnificent since you can see all three falls at once.

Maid of the Mist: This boat trip brings you right up to the foot of the Falls, so you can feel the mist and hear the thunder of the water. It's a memorable experience.

Journey Under the Falls: This attraction brings you down into tunnels behind the Falls, where you can witness the water crashing down from above. You'll even get to stand on a platform very near the Falls.

Niagara Fallsview Casino Resort: This is one of Canada's best casino resorts, with over 3,000 slot machines, 130 gaming tables, and a poker room. It also contains a choice of restaurants and pubs, as well as a theater that presents regular live acts.

Skylon Tower: This tower provides amazing views of the Falls and the surrounding region from its observation deck, which is 775 feet above the earth. It also features a rotating restaurant that serves exquisite dining with panoramic views.

Niagara Parks Butterfly Conservatory: This indoor attraction is home to approximately 2,000 butterflies from throughout the globe, as well as a selection of other exotic insects and plants.

Clifton Hill: This is the primary entertainment sector in Niagara Falls, offering a broad selection of activities, including haunted homes, wax museums, mini golf, and more.

Niagara-on-the-Lake: This attractive town is only a short drive from Niagara Falls and is noted for its gorgeous streets, boutique shops, and vineyards. It's a terrific area to spend a day exploring.

There are many additional sights in and around Niagara Falls, but these are some of the must-sees. Each one gives a distinct viewpoint on this great natural beauty, and they all combine to make Niagara Falls a really memorable vacation.

Tourists activities at Niagara Falls
There are a plethora of exciting things to do at Niagara Falls, and it's not just about taking in the beautiful vistas of the falls themselves. From exhilarating activities to more relaxing hobbies, there is something for everyone.

One of the most popular tourist activities is taking a boat cruise on the Maid of the Mist. This classic boat trip brings you right up to the foot of the falls, where you can feel the mist on your face and hear the thunder of the water. It's an incredible experience that is likely to leave you in amazement.

For a more adrenaline-fueled encounter, there are various possibilities. You may go zip-lining above the Niagara Gorge, or take a helicopter trip for a bird's eye perspective of the falls. There's even the possibility to go bungee jumping if you're feeling brave.

If you're seeking a more casual approach to appreciate the falls, there are lots of alternatives for that as well. You may take a leisurely walk along the Niagara Parkway, which gives beautiful views of the falls and the surrounding environment. You may also take a bike excursion, or hire a kayak or canoe to explore the Niagara River.

For individuals interested in history, there are various museums and historic places to visit. The Niagara Falls History Museum gives an in-depth look at the history of the falls and the surrounding region, while the Niagara Falls Illumination Tower provides a fascinating insight into the technology behind the stunning nightly light displays.

There are also lots of family-friendly attractions, such as the Niagara SkyWheel, a 175-foot Ferris wheel with breathtaking views of the falls, or the Niagara Falls Butterfly Conservatory, where you can witness hundreds of butterflies in a tropical atmosphere. No matter what your hobbies are, there are lots of things to do in Niagara Falls. It's a location where natural beauty and exhilarating adventures come together to create a memorable vacation.

Shopping and Dining in Niagara Falls

Much like other large towns in Ontario, Niagara Falls has a lot to offer when it comes to eating and shopping. Whether you're in the mood for a sophisticated dining experience or a quick bite to eat, Niagara Falls offers it all.

One of the must-visit destinations for foodies in Niagara Falls is the Niagara Fallsview Casino Resort, which boasts several eating choices that appeal to diverse tastes and budgets. The resort has restaurants such as 21 Club Steak and Seafood, Ponte Vecchio, and The Grand Buffet, where tourists can enjoy anything from high-end steaks and seafood to Italian cuisine and all-you-can-eat buffets.

For those who prefer a relaxed eating experience, Clifton Hill is a terrific alternative. The region is home to various fast-food franchises, such as Burger King and KFC, as well as local businesses, such as

Johnny Rocco's Italian Grill and The Beer Garden. Tourists may have a quick meal before moving off to their next activity.

When it comes to shopping, Niagara Falls boasts a range of alternatives, ranging from novelty stores to high-end boutiques. The major retail center is situated on Clifton Hill, where tourists can get anything from T-shirts and magnets to jewelry and apparel. For those who like high-end shopping, the adjacent Niagara-on-the-Lake is home to various shops, such as Mori Gardens and Maison Apothecare, that provide premium items and unusual treasures.

Another fantastic shopping option is the Outlet Collection at Niagara, which has over 100 brand-name retailers, such as Nike, Coach, and Tommy Hilfiger. Guests may catch excellent savings on apparel, shoes, and accessories while enjoying the lovely outdoor mall.

Niagara Falls is not only a terrific destination for its natural beauty but also for its rich food scene and retail opportunities. Tourists may enjoy anything from gourmet dining to fast cuisine, and buy everything from souvenirs to luxury products.

Chapter 5

Other Cities and Regions

As much as Ontario is recognized for its busy metropolis, it is also home to attractive villages and areas ready to be explored. From the lovely vineyards of Niagara-on-the-Lake to the rough wildness of Algonquin Park, there is something for everyone. In this chapter, we will take a tour of some of Ontario's most interesting sites. We will tour the natural splendor of Muskoka, Thousand Islands, and Algonquin Park, discover the picturesque villages of Kingston and Prince Edward County, and enjoy the urban appeal of London and Hamilton. So sit back, relax, and get ready to uncover the hidden beauties that Ontario has to offer.

Kingston:
Situated in Eastern Ontario, Kingston is noted for its rich history and lovely shoreline. The city served as the first capital

of Canada and contains a variety of historic buildings that tourists may explore, including Fort Henry, the Kingston Prison, and the City Hall. Kingston is also home to Queen's University, which is located in the center of the city and is recognized for its gorgeous campus. The waterfront area is a popular place for visitors and residents alike, with a variety of restaurants, cafés, and stores along the streets. Tourists may take a stroll along the boardwalk, hire a bike or a kayak, or just relax and take in the gorgeous landscape.

Hamilton:
Situated between Toronto and Niagara Falls, Hamilton is a city that sometimes goes forgotten by visitors. Yet, the city has a lot to offer, including magnificent parks, waterfalls, and hiking routes. One of the biggest attractions of Hamilton is the Royal Botanical Gardens, which is home to a diversity of flora and animals. Tourists may also explore the city's art culture by visiting

the Art Museum of Hamilton or having a walk through the James Street North arts neighborhood. People interested in history may visit the Canadian Warplane Heritage Museum or the Dundurn National Historic Site.

London:

Situated in southwestern Ontario, London is a vibrant city that is home to a variety of attractions. One of the primary attractions is the Fanshawe Pioneer Village, which is a living history museum that exhibits life in the 19th century. The city is also home to a variety of magnificent parks, including Victoria Park, which boasts a gorgeous fountain and a bandshell that offers concerts throughout the summer. London is also recognized for its arts and cultural scene, with a multitude of festivals and events taking place throughout the year. Visitors may explore the Museum London, which includes a collection of regional art and antiques, or see a performance at the Grand Theatre.

Muskoka:
Muskoka is a scenic area situated in central Ontario, noted for its spectacular natural beauty and the various outdoor activities it provides. With over 1,600 lakes and unending woods, Muskoka is a refuge for nature lovers and outdoor enthusiasts. The area is home to various hiking routes, including the famed Muskoka Trail Network, which encompasses over 400 kilometers of trails. In addition to hiking, guests may also enjoy boating, fishing, camping, and golfing in Muskoka. The area is also famed for its attractive towns and villages, such as Bracebridge, Gravenhurst, and Huntsville, which are studded with quaint shops, galleries, and restaurants.

Algonquin Park
Algonquin Park is a huge wilderness region situated in the middle of Ontario. The park

is famous for its rocky terrain, crystal-clear lakes, and virgin woods. Spanning an area of over 7,600 square kilometers, Algonquin Park is home to a rich assortment of animals, including moose, black bears, wolves, and beavers. Visitors to the park may enjoy many outdoor activities, including hiking, camping, canoeing, and fishing. There are also several beautiful drives in the park, such as the Highway 60 Corridor, which gives spectacular views of the area's surroundings.

Niagara-on-the-Lake

Niagara-on-the-Lake is a lovely hamlet situated in the Niagara Region of Ontario, only a short drive from Niagara Falls. The town is recognized for its medieval architecture, magnificent gardens, and wineries. Tourists may meander through the town's picturesque streets and observe the well-maintained 19th-century structures. Niagara-on-the-Lake is also home to various vineyards, where tourists may enjoy wine tastings and tours. The village is surrounded by lovely scenery, which may be explored on foot, bike, or horseback.

In terms of natural resources, Muskoka and Algonquin Park are noted for their huge woods, pure lakes, and diversified animals. Niagara-on-the-Lake is noted for its wineries and gorgeous gardens.

Chapter 6

Outdoor activities and adventures in the region.

Ontario features a plethora of parks, lakes, and woods, giving the ideal playground for outdoor lovers. From hiking and camping in the lush woods to kayaking and canoeing on the calm lakes, Ontario offers a plethora of outdoor activities to offer.

In this chapter, we will explore some of the most fascinating and adventurous outdoor activities and experiences that Ontario has to offer. Whether you are a seasoned explorer or a novice, we have something for you. So, suit up and get ready for a memorable time in the wonderful outdoors of Ontario.

Hiking and Camping

When you walk into the lush woods of Ontario, the towering trees and eerie quiet may send chills down your spine. But worry not, because the beauty and adventure that await you will make it all worth it.

Hiking and camping in Ontario are not for the faint of heart. The difficult terrain and unexpected weather may make for a tough and fascinating adventure. Yet for those prepared to face the weather, the benefits are beyond measure.

As you journey through the deep woodlands, you will see a broad assortment of species, from towering moose to secretive bears. The crackling of leaves underfoot and the rustling of trees in the wind will be your constant companions as you travel through the woods.

At night, when you huddle around a campfire, the darkness will swallow you, and the howling of wolves in the distance will send shivers down your spine. Yet as you stare up at the starry sky, you will be amazed by the majesty of the cosmos, and a sensation of awe and wonder will sweep over you.

Thus, if you are seeking an adventure that will push your boundaries and leave you breathless, hiking and camping in Ontario is an experience not to be missed. But be cautious, the beauty of the woods is equaled only by its raw and unbridled strength. The wilderness of Ontario is both gorgeous and brutal, and for those who dare to explore it, the rewards may be both scary and exciting. When you head out on your hiking and camping expedition, the thick woods and rocky terrain will test your strength and perseverance. Yet the adrenaline rush of walking through the untamed nature and the breathtaking beauty that surrounds you will make every step worth it.

One of the most recognized hiking places in Ontario is the Bruce Trail. This 900-kilometer track extends from Niagara to Tobermory, carrying walkers through some of the most magnificent landscapes in the province. The track is not for the faint of heart, since it contains tough terrain and high inclines. Yet for those who continue, the sweeping vistas of Lake Huron and Georgian Bay are a spectacular sight.

For those searching for a more private camping experience, Algonquin Park is a must-visit site. This huge park spans almost 7,000 square kilometers of rough nature, including lush woods, dazzling lakes, and steep mountains. The park provides a variety of camping possibilities, from wilderness sites accessible only by canoe or hiking, to drive-in campsites that offer a blend of isolation and convenience.

But be advised, camping in Algonquin Park is not for the faint of heart. The park is home to a variety of species, including moose, bears, and wolves. When you sit around your campfire at night, the howling of wolves in the distance will send shivers down your spine. With its breathtaking beauty and untamed nature, Ontario is a playground for those who dare to explore it.

Skiing and Snowboarding

When the cold of winter sets in, the untamed landscapes of Ontario change into a playground for thrill-seekers. Skiing and snowboarding in Ontario are not for the faint of heart, as the rough terrain and unexpected weather can make for a tough and exhilarating experience.

One of the most prominent skiing areas in Ontario is Blue Mountain. This ski resort has 43 tracks of varied difficulty levels, ranging from mild beginning slopes to steep and demanding lines for the most experienced skiers and snowboarders. Yet the true pleasure of Blue Mountain lies in its night skiing when the eerie light of the snow and the dark woodlands create a frightening environment.

Another popular skiing spot is Mount St. Louis Moonstone. This ski resort features 36 slopes, 9 chairlifts, and 3 carpets, giving plenty of alternatives for skiers and snowboarders of all abilities. Yet it's the steep and tight chutes that will get your adrenaline pounding and leave you breathless.

But be careful, skiing and snowboarding in Ontario may be a perilous activity. The severe winter weather and unexpected terrain may pose a major danger to even the most experienced skiers and snowboarders. The frightening calm of the trees and the eerie brightness of the snow may contribute to the feeling of danger and adventure. If you're seeking an adventure that will leave you both chilly and interested, skiing and snowboarding in Ontario is an experience not to be missed. With its difficult terrain and unpredictable weather, Ontario is a playground for those who dare to battle the elements.

Watersports and Activities

Ontario is a water lover's dream with its many lakes, rivers, and waterways that provide a broad selection of fun water sports and activities. These are some of the greatest sites to enjoy these exhilarating activities in Ontario:

Georgian Bay - This gorgeous harbor situated on the eastern shore of Lake Huron is a favorite site for boating, sailing, and kayaking. Its tranquil waters and lovely environment make it an excellent destination for novices and families.

Thousand Islands - Situated on the St. Lawrence River, the Thousand Islands is a popular site for boating, kayaking, and fishing. The region has over 1,800 islands and is home to various resorts and marinas.

Algonquin Provincial Park - This park is a popular site for canoeists and kayakers, having nearly 2,000 km of canoe routes across its various lakes and rivers. The park also provides several campsites at the water's edge for those who wish to prolong their visit.

Lake Superior - This large lake is famed for its crystal-clear waters and craggy shores, making it a great location for swimming, fishing, and kayaking. The region is also home to various hiking routes and magnificent lookouts.

Niagara River - This river provides an adrenaline-pumping experience for anyone wishing to experience the excitement of white-water kayaking or rafting. The rapids vary from Class II to Class VI, giving a challenge for expert paddlers.

Wasaga Beach - This famous beach on Georgian Bay is the longest freshwater beach in the world and provides several water sports such as swimming, paddle boarding, and jet skiing. It's also home to several coastal stores and eateries.

Lake Simcoe - This big lake situated north of Toronto is a great destination for boating, fishing, and water skiing. Its beautiful waters and tranquil conditions make it perfect for families and novices.

Ontario's lakes, rivers, and waterways provide a broad selection of thrilling water sports and activities for all ages and ability levels. Whether it's kayaking through Algonquin Provincial Park, boating on Georgian Bay, or swimming at Wasaga Beach, there's something for everyone to enjoy in Ontario's magnificent waterways.

Golfing

Golfing is a popular pastime in Ontario, with its scenic scenery and magnificent golf courses drawing golf fans from all over the globe. Here is all you need to know about golfing in Ontario:

Golf Courses:

Ontario is home to numerous world-class golf courses that provide a demanding game and stunning vistas. Some of the finest courses are the Angus Glen Golf Club, situated just north of Toronto, the Glen Abbey Golf Club in Oakville, and the Royal Ontario Golf Club in Milton.

Golf Resorts:

There are several golf resorts in Ontario that appeal to golf aficionados. These resorts provide a range of services such as spas, fine dining restaurants, and luxury hotels. Some of the most popular golf resorts in Ontario are the Muskoka Bay Resort in Gravenhurst, the Deerhurst Resort in Huntsville, and the Millcroft Hotel and Spa in Caledon.

Golf Tournaments:

Ontario holds various golf events throughout the year, drawing players from across the globe. The most renowned event is the RBC Canadian Open, which takes place in June and features some of the greatest names in golf.

Golf Academies:
For those wishing to improve their game, Ontario is home to various golf academies and training facilities. These facilities provide lessons and training programs for golfers of all ability levels, with qualified instructors and state-of-the-art equipment to help improve your swing.

Golfing in Nature:
One of the distinctive characteristics of golfing in Ontario is its gorgeous natural surroundings. Several golf courses are situated in picturesque places such as the Muskoka region, affording spectacular vistas of lakes, woods, and rolling hills.

Fishing
Fishing is a popular sport in Ontario, with its many lakes, rivers, and streams providing some of the greatest fishing in

North America. Here's all you need to know about fishing in Ontario:

Types of Fish:
Ontario is home to a varied variety of fish species, including bass, pike, musky, walleye, trout, salmon, and many more. Each species has its distinct habitat and demands particular strategies to capture, making fishing in Ontario an interesting and hard experience.

Fishing Seasons:
The fishing season in Ontario varies based on the species and the area. Typically, the fishing season begins in May and extends until October. Nevertheless, other species, such as trout and salmon, have distinct seasons that change based on the locality.

Fishing Regulations:
Ontario has rigorous fishing restrictions that safeguard the sustainability of fish populations and the preservation of the

environment. These rules include catch limitations, size restrictions, and conservation initiatives to conserve endangered species.

Fishing Licenses:
To fish in Ontario, you need a valid fishing license. There are numerous permits available, including yearly, seasonal, and daily licenses, and they may be acquired online or through local outfitters.

Fishing Guides:
For those new to fishing or unfamiliar with the region, hiring a fishing guide is a fantastic method to learn about the local fish species and tactics. Fishing guides give experienced expertise, equipment, and access to some of the greatest fishing places in Ontario.

Fishing Lodges:
Fishing lodges are a popular alternative for individuals who wish to combine fishing with a peaceful holiday. These lodges provide comfortable rooms, tasty meals, and access to adjacent fishing sites, making them a perfect option for families and groups of friends.

Ice Fishing:
In the winter, Ontario's lakes and rivers freeze over, giving a unique ice fishing experience. Ice fishing is a popular hobby in Ontario, and several outfitters provide guided trips and equipment rentals.

Fishing in Ontario is a popular and fascinating pastime, with its broad selection of fish species and magnificent natural settings. Whether you're a seasoned fisherman or a newbie, Ontario's lakes, rivers, and streams provide some of the greatest fishing in North America. With rigorous restrictions, professional guides, and luxurious lodges, Ontario is the ideal location for any fishing enthusiast.

Chapter 7

Culture and Arts

When you visit Ontario's bustling cities and attractive communities, you'll uncover a flourishing arts and culture scene that is as varied as it is engaging. From world-class museums to bustling music festivals, Ontario provides something for everyone who values the arts. Join us on a tour around the province's diverse cultural environment and explore the numerous ways in which Ontario expresses itself via art, music, dance, and more. Whether you're a seasoned art fan or simply eager to experience something new, you're sure to be amazed by the beauty and inventiveness of Ontario's arts and culture sector.

Festivals and events

Ontario is host to various festivals and events that exhibit the province's unique culture and rich history. From music festivals to cuisine events, these are some of the greatest festivals and events in Ontario:

The Toronto International Film Festival (TIFF) is one of the most prominent film festivals in the world, drawing filmmakers, industry professionals, and movie enthusiasts from across the globe. The event takes place yearly in Toronto, Ontario, generally during the first two weeks of September. Established in 1976, the festival has developed into a significant cultural event, including hundreds of films from across the globe and drawing over 480,000 spectators in 2019. The festival exhibits a varied spectrum of films, from independent and art-house flicks to big-budget Hollywood blockbusters, and has a reputation for exhibiting some of the most eagerly anticipated films of the year.

One of the distinctive elements of TIFF is its concentration on international filmmaking, with a special emphasis on films from

Africa, Asia, and the Middle East. The festival also incorporates a variety of special programs and events, including panel discussions, Q&A sessions with directors, and a special showing of vintage films.

The festival takes place in different sites in Toronto, including the TIFF Bell Lightbox, a state-of-the-art cinema complex that serves as the festival's headquarters. Additional locations include the Princess of Wales Theatre, the Roy Thomson Hall, and the Scotiabank Theatre Toronto.

One of the highlights of the festival is the red-carpet events when celebrities and filmmakers walk the red carpet before the premiere of their movies. These events are generally highly anticipated, with fans and journalists coming to the locations to get a peek at their favorite performers.

In addition to screening films, TIFF also conducts a variety of industry events and seminars, offering chances for filmmakers and industry professionals to network and learn from each other. The festival also gives a number of honors, including the People's Choice Award, which is voted on by attendees and has become a crucial signal of a film's future success in the broader market.

The Canadian National Exhibition (CNE), popularly known as "The Ex", is an annual exposition that takes place in Toronto, Ontario. The fair normally runs for 18 days in late August and early September and draws over 1.5 million people each year. It is regarded to be one of the biggest fairs in Canada and is commonly referred to as the "Great Canadian Fair".

The CNE has been a mainstay in Toronto since its debut in 1879. Throughout the years, it has developed into a major entertainment event, with a broad array of attractions and activities for all ages. Some of the most popular activities at the fair are midway, which has a number of rides and games, as well as the Canadian International Air Show, which takes place over Labour Day weekend and shows a range of aerial acrobatics and displays.

Other popular attractions at the CNE include the food building, which exhibits a broad selection of unusual and tasty cuisines from across the globe, and the exposition hall, which shows the newest goods and advancements in a number of sectors. There are also a multitude of concerts, performances, and special events that take place during the fair, including celebrity appearances, parades, and contests.

One of the most popular attractions of the CNE is the legendary "Prize House" contest, in which visitors may buy tickets for a chance to win a completely equipped home, complete with appliances and furniture. The prize house is a key lure for tourists and has become a treasured tradition at the fair.

In addition to being a major entertainment event, the CNE also plays an essential role in the community, supporting local companies and creating chances for employment and entrepreneurship. The fair is operated by the Canadian National Exhibition Association, a non-profit organization that strives to promote and support the fair and its affiliated events and activities.

Overall, the Canadian National Exhibition is a cherished and much-anticipated event in Toronto, offering something for everyone and giving a unique and exciting way to commemorate the end of summer.

Ottawa tulip Festival
The Ottawa Tulip Festival is an annual celebration of spring and the beauty of tulips. The event takes place in Ottawa, the capital city of Canada, often in May. The

event has a long and rich history, going back to 1945 when the Dutch royal family brought 100,000 tulip bulbs to Ottawa as a sign of appreciation for Canada's involvement in the liberation of the Netherlands during World War II.

Since then, the Ottawa Tulip Festival has developed into one of the biggest tulip festivals in the world, drawing over 600,000 people each year. The celebration displays approximately one million tulips in bloom around the city, in public gardens, parks, and other public areas. The tulips come in a broad range of colors and designs, providing a gorgeous and vivid display that is a wonderful feast for the eyes.

In addition to the tulip displays, the festival also provides a broad selection of events and activities for guests of all ages. They include guided tours of the tulip displays, live music performances, art exhibitions, street performances, and more. The event also has a range of food and drink exhibitors, delivering tasty delights and drinks from across the globe. One of the most popular activities of the Ottawa Tulip Festival is the Tulipmania Fireworks show, which takes place over Dow's Lake and involves a magnificent display of pyrotechnics matched to the music. The fireworks show is a popular tradition and attracts enormous audiences from throughout the city and beyond. The Ottawa Tulip Festival is also a celebration of the cultural links between Canada and the Netherlands and involves a variety of unique activities and displays reflecting the history and culture of the Netherlands. This features performances by Dutch musicians and dancers, displays of Dutch art and history, and a unique "Dutch Market" exhibiting real Dutch goods and products.

Ultimately, the Ottawa Tulip Festival is a celebration of spring, beauty, and cultural interaction, and is a cherished and much-anticipated event in Ottawa and beyond.

Stratford Festival

The Stratford Festival is an annual festival of theater and the performing arts that takes place in Stratford, Ontario, Canada. The festival normally runs from late April to early November and incorporates a broad variety of works, including plays, musicals, operas, and other types of live performances. The Stratford Festival was created in 1953 by Tom Patterson, a journalist and theatrical lover who dreamt of developing a world-class theater festival in Canada. The festival was primarily centered on the works of William Shakespeare, and its debut production was a performance of "Richard III" with Alec Guinness in the main role.

Since then, the Stratford Festival has developed into one of the biggest and most acclaimed theatrical festivals in the world, drawing over 500,000 people each year. The festival offers performances of classic and current plays, as well as new works commissioned particularly for the event. Performances are produced in a number of locations, including the Festival Theatre, the Avon Theatre, the Tom Patterson Theatre, and the Studio Theatre.

In addition to its mainstage plays, the Stratford Festival also provides a broad variety of additional events and activities. They include discussions and lectures by theatrical professionals, backstage tours of the festival's facilities, and a range of special activities and workshops for theater aficionados of all ages. The Stratford Festival is noted for its dedication to quality in all elements of theatrical production, including acting, directing, design, and technical execution. The festival draws some of the world's most gifted performers, directors, and designers, and has started the careers of many of Canada's most prominent theatrical professionals. The Stratford Festival is a celebration of the performing arts, a showcase for some of the world's top theatrical plays, and a renowned cultural institution in Canada and abroad. It is a must-visit location for everyone with a passion for theater and the arts.

Canadian Music Week

Canadian Music Week (CMW) is an annual music festival and industry conference that takes place in Toronto, Canada. The festival normally runs for five days in May and showcases a varied spectrum of music genres and styles, including rock, hip-hop, pop, electronic, and more.

The festival was launched in 1981 as the Canadian Music Industry Conference and has since developed into one of the biggest and most prominent music events in North America, gathering over 3,000 musicians and industry executives from across the globe. The festival's major emphasis is on new artists, giving them a platform to display their abilities and engage with industry experts, fans, and other musicians.

CMW is also noted for its industry conference, which contains keynote speakers, panel discussions, and networking opportunities for music professionals. The conference covers a broad variety of issues, including music creation and distribution, marketing and promotion, copyright and intellectual property, and more. The conference gathers some of the largest names in the music business, offering guests unique insights and the opportunity to meet with industry professionals. In addition to the primary festival and conference events, CMW also incorporates a number of additional activities and programs. They include awards presentations, film screenings, comedy acts, and more. The festival also works with local companies and venues to offer events and parties across the city, providing a dynamic and exciting scene for music enthusiasts and industry professionals alike. It's a celebration of the finest in developing music, a great platform for industry professionals to interact and learn, and a must-attend event for anybody with a passion for music and the music business.

Toronto Caribbean Carnival
The Toronto Caribbean Carnival, often known as Caribana, is an annual cultural celebration that celebrates Caribbean culture and customs. The event takes place in Toronto, Canada, throughout the summer and normally continues for three weeks, concluding in a big procession that attracts nearly a million attendees.

The festival started in 1967 as a celebration of Canada's centennial year and the Caribbean community's cultural legacy. Nowadays, the festival has become one of the major cultural events in North America, drawing over a million attendees each year and providing a broad variety of programs and activities. One of the attractions of the Toronto Caribbean Carnival is the procession, which incorporates spectacular costumes, music, and dance acts. The parade route goes through the streets of Toronto and is crowded with onlookers who come to witness the colorful floats and performers.

In addition to the parade, the festival also incorporates a range of other events and activities, including music, food and drink tastings, arts and crafts exhibitions, and more. Guests may enjoy traditional Caribbean food, listen to live music from famous Caribbean artists, and learn about the culture and customs of the Caribbean community. The event also features a Junior Carnival for children, giving them a chance to demonstrate their creativity and cultural pride via costume and dance performances.

Niagara Wine Festival

The Niagara Wine Festival is an annual festival of wine and winemaking that takes place in the Niagara area of Ontario, Canada. The event is normally held in September and celebrates the region's world-class wines and vineyards. The event started in 1952 as a tiny grape and wine festival and has since developed into one of the major wine festivals in Canada, with over 100,000 attendees each year. The festival's major emphasis is on presenting the greatest wines of the Niagara area and teaching visitors about the art of winemaking. The festival features the Exploration Pass program, which enables guests to try wines and food combinations at participating wineries around the Niagara area. The festival also incorporates a number of additional events and activities, including vineyard tours, grape stomping contests, and seminars on wine tasting and food matching.

The festival's centerpiece event is the Grand Parade, which incorporates colorful floats, live music, and marching bands. The procession passes through the streets of downtown St. Catharines, the center of the Niagara wine region, and is a highlight of the festival for many tourists. In addition to the events and activities, the Niagara Wine Festival also offers a chance for visitors to learn about the history and culture of the Niagara area, including its indigenous roots and the significance of wine to the local economy. It is a celebration of the Niagara region's rich wine culture and gives visitors a chance to tour the region's magnificent vineyards, drink world-class wines, and enjoy the warm hospitality of the local winemakers.

Taste of Toronto
Taste of Toronto is an annual cuisine event that takes place in Toronto, Canada. The event brings together some of the city's greatest chefs, restaurants, and food artists,

offering visitors a unique chance to enjoy a broad variety of culinary masterpieces. The event normally takes place over four days in June and showcases over 50 of the city's greatest restaurants, providing everything from quick snacks to full-course dinners. Guests may buy food and drink tickets to taste meals from various restaurants and experience different wines, beers, and cocktails. In addition to the cuisine, Taste of Toronto also provides a variety of culinary experiences and activities, including cooking demos, wine tastings, and seminars on themes like food photography and food styling. The event also features a selection of live entertainment, including music and comedy shows.

One of the attractions of Taste of Toronto is the chance to meet and connect with some of the city's best chefs and food industry experts. Guests may see demos by their favorite chefs and learn about their culinary skills and inspiration. Taste of Toronto also gives a chance to learn about the varied culinary scene in Toronto and the numerous cultural influences that have created the city's food culture. From traditional Canadian food to cosmopolitan delicacies, travelers may discover the vast diversity of culinary traditions represented in the city. Taste of Toronto is a must-visit place for food enthusiasts and anybody interested in experiencing the flourishing culinary scene in Toronto.

Festival of Lights

The Festival of Lights is an annual event that takes place in Niagara Falls, Ontario, Canada. The event runs from November through January and incorporates an assortment of light displays, music, and entertainment for guests of all ages. The event contains over three million lights, transforming Niagara Falls into a stunning display of color and light. The light displays feature everything from typical Christmas themes to more innovative displays, such as enormous lit sculptures and animated light shows.

In addition to the light displays, the Festival of Lights also incorporates a range of entertainment and events, including live music concerts, fireworks displays, and a Christmas market. Tourists may also take a trip on the Niagara SkyWheel, a large Ferris wheel that gives amazing views of the light shows and the falls.

One main attraction of the Festival of Lights is the Niagara Falls Illumination, which takes place each night throughout the event. The falls are lighted with a dazzling rainbow of colors, producing a spectacular show of light and water. The Festival of Lights also allows tourists the chance to explore the Niagara Falls area and its various attractions, including the Niagara Falls State Park, the Niagara Falls Butterfly Conservatory, and the Niagara Fallsview Casino Resort.

Overall, the Festival of Lights is a spectacular and joyful event that allows tourists a unique chance to see the splendor of Niagara Falls in a fresh and compelling manner. It is a must-visit site for everyone wishing to get into the Christmas mood and appreciate the beauty of nature and light.

Art and Architecture

Ontario is a treasure trove of art and architecture, with a varied variety of styles and influences on exhibit across the province. These are some of the important highlights:

Art Galleries: Ontario has a vibrant art gallery culture, containing everything from classic and modern art to photography and sculpture. Some of the most renowned galleries are the Art Gallery of Ontario in Toronto, the McMichael Canadian Art Collection in Kleinburg, and the National Gallery of Canada in Ottawa.

Public Art: Ontario is also home to a multitude of public artworks, ranging from sculptures and murals to interactive installations and performance art. Some of the most notable public art projects in the province are the Aga Khan Museum in Toronto, the Monument to Canadian Relief Workers in Ottawa, and the Light Showers artwork in Niagara Falls.

Architecture: Ontario possesses a rich architectural past, with buildings ranging from medieval Gothic Revival architecture to contemporary marvels. Some of the most noteworthy examples are the Parliament Buildings in Ottawa, the CN Tower in Toronto, and the Royal Ontario Museum in Toronto, which boasts a spectacular crystal-like extension.

Historic Sites: Ontario is home to a range of historic sites and structures, including historical forts, heritage residences, and monuments that have played an important part in creating the province's history. Some of the more renowned sites are the Fort Henry National Historic Site in Kingston, Casa Loma in Toronto, and the Rideau Canal National Historic Site in Ottawa.

Street Art: Ontario's cities are also home to a flourishing street art culture, with murals and graffiti covering buildings and alleys around the province. Some of the more notable examples are the brilliant graffiti art in Toronto's Kensington Market and the colorful murals in the St. Clair West district of Toronto.

Ontario is a center of art and architecture, providing a varied variety of styles and influences for tourists to discover and appreciate. From public art projects to ancient locations to modernist masterpieces, Ontario offers something for everyone to enjoy and adore.

Chapter 8

Food and Drinks

Welcome to the chapter on food and beverages in Ontario! Get ready to indulge in a gastronomic adventure as we take you on a tour around Ontario's varied and wonderful food scene. Ontario is a melting pot of cultures and influences, and nowhere is this more obvious than in its food and drink choices. From farm-to-table meals and artisanal cheeses to craft beer and award-winning wines, Ontario offers something for every palette. Whether you're a gourmet searching out the newest culinary trends or just wanting to sample some of the greatest local flavors, Ontario's food and drink culture is guaranteed to excite and surprise you. Now let's take a fork and get in!

Local cuisine

Local cuisine is at the center of Ontario's food scene, displaying the province's copious agricultural resources and rich culinary tradition. Ontario's chefs and restaurateurs are enthusiastic about utilizing locally-sourced ingredients to produce inventive and delectable meals that represent the region's distinct tastes and traditions.

One of the distinguishing elements of Ontario's native cuisine is its focus on farm-to-table eating. Several of the province's greatest restaurants work closely with local farmers and producers to get fresh, seasonal products that are typically farmed or cultivated within a few miles from the kitchen. From luscious Niagara peaches and crisp apples to delicate meat and exquisite cheeses, Ontario's local food is all about savoring the region's natural riches.

Another trademark of Ontario's unique cuisine is its ethnic influences. With a diversified population that includes individuals from all over the globe, Ontario's culinary scene is a melting pot of tastes and customs. From spicy Indian curries and aromatic Thai soups to substantial Italian pasta and smokey Southern Barbecue, Ontario's unique cuisine provides a world of pleasures for tourists to enjoy.

And let's not forget about Ontario's hallmark foods, which are a must-try for every gourmet visiting the province. From butter tarts and poutine to peameal bacon sandwiches and Niagara icewine, Ontario's gastronomic pleasures are as varied as they are delectable.

Perhaps you're exploring the farmers' markets of Toronto, relishing a farm-to-table dinner in Prince Edward County, or sinking into a hearty dish of poutine in Ottawa, Ontario's local cuisine is a feast for the senses that is guaranteed to thrill and inspire. So come hungry and be ready to enjoy the pleasures of Ontario's distinct and excellent local food.

Below are five excellent restaurants in Ontario where you may experience wonderful local cuisine:

- Canoe Restaurant & Bar, Toronto: Situated on the 54th level of the TD Bank Tower, Canoe Restaurant and Bar provides stunning views of Toronto's cityscape with a menu of modern Canadian cuisine. The cuisine varies with the seasons, presenting the greatest local foods and tastes.

- Langdon Hall Country House Hotel & Spa, Cambridge: Situated on a lovely rural estate, Langdon Hall provides a sumptuous dining experience offering farm-to-table food produced with ingredients acquired from the hotel's gardens and neighboring farms.

- The Restaurant at Pearl Morissette, Niagara-on-the-Lake: The Restaurant at Pearl Morissette provides a unique and original dining experience that mixes French and Canadian cuisine with an emphasis on natural wines. The menu varies often to reflect the greatest local foods and tastes.

- Feast On certified restaurants: The Feast On accreditation is a program that rewards restaurants in Ontario that employ local, seasonal, and sustainable foods. Some of the top Feast On accredited restaurants are North and Navy in Ottawa, Backhouse in Niagara-on-the-Lake, and Actinolite in Toronto.

- Treadwell Farm-to-Table Cuisine, Port Dalhousie: Treadwell Farm-to-Table Cuisine is a beautiful restaurant set in the historic Lakeside Hotel in Port Dalhousie. The cuisine highlights locally-sourced delicacies from the Niagara area, including fresh fish and artisanal cheeses.

Each of these restaurants gives a distinct and delectable flavor of Ontario's native cuisine, making them a must-visit for foodies and anybody eager to experience the province's culinary delights.

Winery and Vineyards
Ontario's growing winery and vineyard scene offers visitors a place where they can enjoy the province's world-class wines, gorgeous landscapes, and rich cultural history. With more than 100 wineries and vineyards dotted around the province, Ontario has become a favorite destination for wine enthusiasts from around the globe.

Ontario's wine sector is best renowned for its cool-climate varieties, including Riesling, Chardonnay, Pinot Noir, and Cabernet Franc. The province's vineyards benefit from a unique mix of rich soils, moderate slopes, and cooling lake breezes that offer perfect growth conditions for various grape varieties. One of the finest ways to see Ontario's winery and vineyard sector is by going on a wine tour. Several of the province's vineyards provide tours and tastings, offering visitors an opportunity to meet the winemakers, learn about the winemaking process, and taste some of Ontario's best wines.

Some of the finest wine areas in Ontario include the Niagara Peninsula, Prince Edward County, and the Lake Erie North Shore. The Niagara Peninsula is undoubtedly the most recognized wine area in Ontario, given its gorgeous vistas, world-class vineyards, and closeness to Toronto. Prince Edward County is another prominent wine area, situated only a few hours east of Toronto and famed for its small wineries and gorgeous vineyards. The Lake Erie North Shore area, situated in southwestern Ontario, is home to several wineries that specialize in cool-climate varietals such as Riesling and Pinot Noir.

In addition to its award-winning wines, Ontario's wineries, and vineyards also provide tourists with an opportunity to explore the province's rich cultural legacy. Several vineyards hold events and festivals throughout the year that showcase Ontario's history, customs, and local food. From grape stomping and harvest celebrations to wine and food pairings, there's always something going on in Ontario's winery and vineyard industry.

Whether you're a seasoned wine enthusiast or just seeking to discover Ontario's gorgeous landscapes and rich culture, the province's winery and vineyard scene is a must-visit destination that is guaranteed to thrill and inspire. Now raise a glass and taste the flavors of Ontario's world-class wines!

Craft beer and Breweries

Craft beer and breweries have risen in popularity in Ontario in recent years, with new microbreweries and taprooms popping up around the province. Ontario's craft beer movement is noted for its inventiveness, innovation, and devotion to utilizing local ingredients and supporting local communities.

One of the main locations for craft beer fans in Ontario is Toronto, which is home to dozens of breweries and taprooms. Some of the most popular breweries in the city are Bellwoods Brewery, Steam Whistle Brewing, and Left Field Brewery. Several of these breweries provide tours and tastings, offering visitors an opportunity to learn about the brewing process and try some of the greatest craft beers in the province.

Outside of Toronto, numerous other locations in Ontario are recognized for their craft beer and breweries. The Niagara Area, for example, is home to several breweries that specialize in utilizing locally-sourced components such as hops and fruit. Some of the most prominent breweries in the area include Silversmith Brewing Company, Oast House Brewers, and Bench Brewing Company. Another famous craft beer destination in Ontario is Ottawa, which has a growing craft beer culture that is focused around the fashionable Hintonburg district. Some of the top breweries in Ottawa are Dominion City Brewing Company, Beyond the Pale Brewing Company, and Tooth and Nail Brewing Company.

In addition to creating great and inventive beers, Ontario's craft brewers are also noted for their dedication to sustainability and community participation. Several brewers adopt environmentally-friendly brewing processes and help local farmers and craftspeople by purchasing their supplies locally. Ontario's craft beer and brewery culture is a lively and fascinating element of the province's gastronomic environment.

Whether you're a beer fan or just seeking to discover the local culture and community, a visit to one of Ontario's craft breweries is a must-do experience that is sure to leave you with a renewed respect for the art and science of brewing.

Food Tours and Tastings
Food tours and tastings have been more popular in Ontario in recent years, with people coming to the province to enjoy its world-class food and various culinary traditions. From gourmet cheeses and cured meats to farm-fresh fruit and sweet maple syrup, Ontario's culinary scene is a feast for the senses.

One of the finest ways to discover Ontario's gastronomic environment is by going on a food tour. Numerous cities in Ontario provide guided culinary tours that take guests to some of the greatest restaurants, cafés, and markets in the region. These excursions sometimes include tastes of local delicacies, such as peameal bacon sandwiches in Toronto or butter tarts in Niagara-on-the-Lake. In addition to city tours, various food and drink excursions concentrate on particular areas or products. For example, travelers may join a wine and cheese tour in Prince Edward County, where they can sample locally-made wines and artisanal cheeses, or go on a craft beer tour in Ottawa, where they can taste some of the province's greatest craft beers.

For those who want a more hands-on culinary experience, there are also numerous cooking lessons and workshops offered around the region. These programs span from fundamental knife skills and baking methods to advanced gourmet cuisine and food pairing. Some of the most prominent culinary schools in Ontario are The Chef Upstairs in Toronto and The Good Earth Food and Wine Company in Niagara-on-the-Lake.

Many of Ontario's finest restaurants and chefs also provide tasting menus that highlight the best of the province's cuisine. These menus generally incorporate local and seasonal products and are combined with wines or craft brews to provide an immersive dining experience. Food tours and tastings are a terrific opportunity to discover the rich and varied culinary traditions of Ontario. A culinary tour or tasting is a must-do event that is sure to leave you with a greater appreciation for Ontario's world-class cuisine.

Chapter 9

Accommodation

Choosing the proper lodging may make all the difference in your trip experience. Whether you're searching for a nice bed & breakfast, a luxurious hotel, or a budget-friendly hostel, Ontario provides a broad selection of lodging alternatives to fit every traveler's requirements and interests. In this chapter, we will walk you through the greatest lodging alternatives in Ontario, from the hectic metropolitan centers of Toronto and Ottawa to the calm countryside of the Niagara area. So sit back, relax, and let us help you find the perfect place to stay during your Ontario adventure.

- The Ritz-Carlton, Toronto: Located in the heart of downtown Toronto, The Ritz-Carlton offers unparalleled luxury with its elegantly appointed rooms and suites, world-class dining options, and impeccable service. The hotel also includes a magnificent spa and fitness facility, as well as breathtaking views of the metropolitan skyline and Lake Ontario.

- Four Seasons Hotel Toronto: Located in the fashionable Yorkville district, the Four Seasons Hotel Toronto provides an elegant refuge with its large rooms and suites, outstanding dining choices, and top-notch facilities, including a full-service spa and indoor pool.

- The Hazelton Hotel, Toronto: With its sleek and modern design, The Hazelton Hotel provides a refined urban sanctuary in the heart of Toronto's posh Yorkville area. The hotel has large rooms and suites, a world-class restaurant, and a magnificent spa, as well as a rooftop lounge with panoramic views of the city.

- Langdon Hall Country House Hotel & Spa, Cambridge: For those seeking a more quiet location, Langdon Hall Country House Hotel & Spa provides an exquisite hideaway in the picturesque countryside of Cambridge, Ontario. The historic resort boasts tastefully designed rooms and suites, outstanding dining choices, and a magnificent spa, as well as wide gardens and nature walks.

- The St. Regis Toronto: This magnificent facility enjoys one of the greatest sites in Toronto, overlooking the renowned CN Tower and Lake Ontario. The St. Regis provides large rooms and suites with breathtaking views, as well as great dining choices, a full-service spa, and a rooftop infinity pool with panoramic views of the city.

Traveling on a budget might be a struggle, but it's not impossible in Ontario. The province provides a choice of economical housing alternatives for people wishing to save money without compromising comfort and convenience. In this area, we will examine the most budget-friendly lodgings in Ontario, from lovely bed & breakfasts to economical hotels and motels. We'll also supply you with some top choices for places to stay that won't break the bank. Therefore, whether you're planning a family holiday, a hiking trip, or a solitary excursion, you'll find plenty of alternatives to select from in Ontario. Let's dig in and explore some of the greatest budget-friendly lodgings in the province.

- HI Toronto Hostel: Located in the heart of downtown Toronto, HI Toronto Hostel offers affordable and comfortable accommodations for budget-conscious travelers. The hostel features clean and cozy dormitory-style rooms, private rooms, a fully-equipped kitchen, and a common area for socializing and meeting other travelers.

- Alexandra Hotel, Toronto: The Alexandra Hotel is a budget-friendly alternative that doesn't compromise location or comfort. Situated in the busy Queen West district, the hotel provides comfortable rooms with basic facilities, free Wi-Fi, and a handy position near many of Toronto's major attractions.

- Comfort Inn, Niagara Falls: The Comfort Inn offers comfortable and affordable accommodation in the heart of Niagara Falls. The motel has clean and cheerful rooms with minimal facilities, a complimentary breakfast, and a handy position only minutes away from the falls.

- Best Western Plus, Ottawa: The Best Western Plus is a budget-friendly alternative in Ottawa that doesn't sacrifice quality or comfort. The hotel provides clean and spacious rooms, a fitness facility, free breakfast, and a convenient position near many of the city's major attractions.

- Westwinds Motel, Tobermory: The Westwinds Motel provides economical accommodation in the picturesque village of Tobermory, recognized for its magnificent natural beauty and outdoor activities. The motel features clean and comfortable rooms, free Wi-Fi, and a convenient location close to the town's many attractions.

Chapter 10

Practical information

As exciting as travel can be, it often requires some planning and preparation to ensure a smooth and stress-free trip. In this chapter, we will give you all the practical information you need to know to make the most of your vacation to Ontario. From transportation and lodgings to currency exchange and visa needs, we've got you covered. So sit back, relax, and let us lead you through the crucial things you need to know before beginning your Ontario vacation.

When traveling in Ontario, it's crucial to be aware of safety problems and have emergency contacts on hand in case of an emergency. Here are some practical ideas to help you remain safe throughout your travels:

Be aware of your environment: Pay attention to your surroundings and trust your intuition. Avoid going alone in unfamiliar or poorly-lit locations at night.

Protect your belongings: Keep your valuables in a safe area and never leave them alone. Be careful of pickpockets and avoid bringing big quantities of money or costly things with you.

Respect local laws and traditions: Be respectful of local laws and customs, especially clothing standards and cultural norms. Familiarize yourself with the rules and regulations of the location you are going.

Be informed: Keep up-to-date on local news and current events, and be aware of any possible safety issues or natural catastrophes that may affect your travels.

In case of an emergency, here are some critical phone numbers to have on hand:

Police, Fire, Ambulance: 911
Ontario   Provincial   Police   (OPP)
Non-Emergency: 1-888-310-1122
Canadian Coast Guard: 1-800-267-7270
Ontario Poison Centre: 1-800-268-9017

It's also a good idea to make note of the contact information for your embassy or consulate, as well as the location of the closest hospital or medical institution. Following these procedures will assist guarantee that you have a safe and happy vacation to Ontario.

Health
It's crucial to take care of your health when vacationing in Ontario. Here are some ideas and information about health and medical services to help you keep well and prepared throughout your trip:

Health Insurance: It's crucial to make sure you have proper health insurance coverage when vacationing in Ontario. Check with your insurance provider to determine whether your coverage covers you while overseas, and consider obtaining supplemental travel health insurance if required.

Vaccinations: Make sure your usual immunizations are up-to-date before flying to Ontario. Based on your travel intentions and medical history, you may additionally require extra immunizations. Speak with your healthcare practitioner or contact a travel health center for help.

Prescription Medications: If you use prescription drugs, ensure you have enough for the length of your vacation. Keep them in their original labeled containers, and bring a copy of your prescription with you in case you need to refill your medicine while overseas.

Medical Facilities: Ontario has a comprehensive healthcare system, with several hospitals and medical clinics spread across the province. In case of an emergency, phone 911 for rapid medical treatment. For non-emergency medical treatment, visit a walk-in clinic or family doctor's office.

Pharmacies: Pharmacies, or drug shops as they are often known in Ontario, are found across the province. Many are open late and on weekends, and

Language and Culture tips
While visiting Ontario, it's necessary to be informed of the local language and cultural norms to completely immerse oneself in the experience. Here are some important suggestions to keep in mind:

Language: The official language of Ontario is English, although French is also widely spoken in some areas. It's usually a good idea to learn a few simple phrases in the local language before your vacation.

Greetings: Canadians are renowned for being nice and inviting, so don't be shocked if you're welcomed with a grin and a warm greeting. A handshake is a common greeting, although close friends and family members may hug or kiss on the cheek.

Tipping: In Canada, it's normal to tip at restaurants, cafés, and other service sectors. A gratuity of 15-20% of the entire price is usual for excellent service.

Etiquette: Canadians are typically polite and respectful, therefore it's crucial to be kind and thoughtful in your dealings with people. Avoid interrupting people while they're speaking, and always say "please" and "thank you".

Dress code: Ontario has a reasonably relaxed dress code, however, it's always a good idea to verify the dress code for any particular events or sites you intend to attend. In general, comfortable and functional attire is good for most activities.

By keeping these cultural ideas in mind, you'll be better prepared to negotiate Ontario's language and traditions and have a more pleasurable and genuine vacation experience.

Helpful websites and applications
Here are some excellent websites and applications to help you plan and enjoy your vacation to Ontario:

Ontario Travel: The official tourist website for Ontario, this site gives information on lodgings, attractions, events, and more. https://www.ontariotravel.net/en/home

Transit: This software lets you navigate public transit in Ontario cities, providing timetables and routes for buses, trains, and subways. https://transitapp.com/

Weather Network: Keep up-to-date on the weather in Ontario with this app, which gives predictions, warnings, and live radar maps.
https://www.theweathernetwork.com/ca/weather/ontario

Google Maps: This software is a must-have for every traveler, delivering precise maps and instructions for navigating Ontario's towns and countryside.
https://www.google.com/maps

Parks Canada: For outdoor lovers, this app gives information on national parks and historic sites in Ontario, including trail maps, camping bookings, and more.
https://www.pc.gc.ca/en/index

Ontario is a place that provides a varied selection of experiences for tourists. From the busy metropolis to the natural beauty of the countryside, there is no lack of things to see and do in this interesting area. Whether

you're interested in discovering
culture and arts scene, enjoying the
excellent food, or immersing yourself in the
gorgeous natural surroundings, Ontario
offers something for everyone.

By utilizing the information given in this
travel guide, you can plan your ideal
vacation to Ontario and make the most of
your stay in this great location. Whether
you're traveling on a budget or searching for
a luxury experience, there are plenty of
lodgings, restaurants, and activities to pick
from.

From the lively nightlife of Toronto to the
tranquil serenity of Lake Huron, Ontario is a
place that will fascinate and inspire you. So
why wait? Start arranging your vacation to
Ontario now and explore everything that
this great area has to offer!

Printed in Great Britain
by Amazon

21872037R00069